STEP INTO NATURE

In Fields and Meadows

Written by Michael Chinery
Illustrated by John Gosler

GRANADA

Published by Granada Publishing 1984
Granada Publishing Limited
8 Grafton Street, London W1X 3LA

Copyright © Templar Publishing Ltd 1984
Illustrations copyright © Templar Publishing Ltd 1984

British Library Cataloguing in Publication Data
Chinery, Michael
   In fields and meadows.– (Step into Nature; 4)
   1. Meadow ecology – Juvenile literature
   I. Title   II. Series
   574.5'2643   QH541.5.M4

   ISBN 0-246-12175-0

Series devised by Richard Carlisle
Edited by Mandy Wood
Designed by Mick McCarthy
Printed in Italy

Contents

No matter where you live, you are surrounded by nature. In the towns, even in the cities, you will find birds and animals, plants and trees, and insects to watch and wonder about. STEP INTO NATURE is about all these things–the everyday creatures as well as the elusive. It's packed with nature projects to do, nature diaries to keep and clues and signs for the nature detective to read. It will teach you how to look at the world of nature around you, how to understand its working and how to conserve it for others.

Life in the fields

Most of Europe was once covered with forest. But a few thousand years ago, people started to cut down the trees to make room for their crops and animals. So now, all these years later, most of the great forests have disappeared and, in their place, are the fields, meadows and other grasslands that have been "made" by man. Each different type of grassland has its own special collection of wildlife, and in the following pages you can find out about some of the fascinating creatures and plants that live out their lives among the grasses.

First, there are the rough grasslands of the hills, grazed by the farmer's sheep. Here you will also find lots of rabbits helping to keep the vegetation short. And, as long as there are not *too* many animals, there will also be plenty of small flowering plants. The slow-growing tree seedlings cannot survive being nibbled, though, so they will not grow while the animals remain. You can read about what happens when the creatures are removed on page 26.

The lower grasslands are mostly divided into fields and used for farming. Often they are treated with fertilisers to make the grass or crops grow better and, as such, are obviously far from being natural habitats. Some fields are grazed by sheep and cattle while others are left to grow up into hay meadows. Huge areas are also used to grow crops, like those in the panel.

The big picture shows some of the wild flowers and animals that live in the rough grasslands all over Britain and Europe. Look for them when you're out walking in the fields or driving past farmland in the car. Make notes of what you see in your *Nature Diary*.

1. Wheatear
2. Kestrel
3. Common blue butterfly
4. Rabbit
5. Mole
6. Snail
7. Grass snake
8. Lapwing
9. Cinnabar moth

Name that cereal!

Cereals cover huge areas of the countryside. They are really just large grasses with nutritious seeds. They are sown in autumn or spring and harvested, usually with huge combine harvesters, in late summer. Four main cereals are grown in Europe. Can you find them all? Several others, including rye and sorghum, are grown on a smaller scale.

Wheat *(left)* is one of the most important cereals in Europe. Its plump grains contain lots of flour which is used for making bread and other food. The ears are usually upright, without long bristles.

Barley *(right)* is grown on a large scale and is used for feeding pigs and other farm animals. A large amount is also used to make beer. The ears are rather flattened, with long bristles, and they hang down when ripe.

Oats *(left)* are grown mainly in the cooler and wetter areas. They are easily recognised by their branching heads, which lack dense ears.

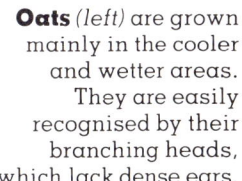

Maize *(right)*, often known as corn, carries its grain in very dense ears called cobs. It grows mainly in the warmer areas and is used for cattle feed.

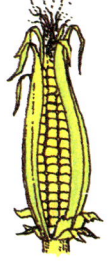

5

The Mad March hare

The best time to watch hares is in early spring. They are out and about during the day at this time of year and often move around in small groups. The males often indulge in spectacular chases, leaping high into the air and even fighting, rather like boxers. You can see two of them in the picture doing just that. All of these activities have led to their having the nickname of "Mad March hares", for it is only during the months of spring that they act this way. At other times of year the animals tend to live alone and become largely nocturnal. You can often see them bounding along the road in front of you if you are in a car at night. They can run very fast.

The hares in the picture are brown hares. There is another kind known as the mountain hare. It has smaller ears than the brown hare and, as its name suggests, it prefers upland areas. It generally turns white in winter. Can you think why? Both hares are closely related to the rabbit. You can discover the differences between them on page 15.

The brown hare lives mainly on farmland, amongst cereals and other crops, as well as on pastureland. It feeds mainly on grass and often damages young cereal crops in the spring. It usually crouches very low when feeding, with its ears almost flat, as you can see in the small picture on the far right. Its large eyes and big ears, combined with a good sense of smell, enable the hare to spot danger from far away. It may then crouch even lower, so that it is very hard to pick out among the grasses, but more often it will rise up on its long legs and bound away.

Unlike the rabbit, the hare does not have its babies in a burrow. The young hares, called *leverets*, are born on a flattened patch of grass called a *form*. Their eyes are open at birth, and they can run about almost straight away.

You can discover the differences between them on page 15.

The hare's tracks

nature watch

The hare's tracks are very easy to find in fields after a fall of snow. Try to follow some of them, to see how far the hare moves in a night. How often does it sit down to rest?

When it's running along, the hare puts its two front feet down with one just in front of the other. It then swings its hind feet forward so that they land almost side by side *in front of the front feet!* You thus get a group of four foot prints arranged as shown below. And, of course, the faster the hare runs, the greater the distance between each group of prints. When the hare sits down for a rest, the back feet leave rather long prints, and just in front of them you'll see the smaller prints of the hare's front feet. The hare's tracks are not easy to see on the ground, unless it is very soft. But the animals tend to use the same routes through the fields and you can often see these because the soil and grass become flattened to form clear paths. The tracks made by rabbits are similar to those of the hare except that they are smaller and closer together.

Front feet   Hind feet Print made by sitting hare

Fairy rings

Have you ever noticed that mushrooms and toadstools often grow in rings? They grow like this in the fields, and on lawns and roadside verges. The rings are called *fairy rings*, but there isn't really anything magical about them. In fact, there's a very simple explanation for why they grow this way.

The toadstools start off growing in a single clump, sprouting from a dense cluster of hair-like threads under the ground. The threads spread out in all directions, feeding on decaying grass roots and other rotting matter in the soil. Eventually, they use up all the food material in the centre of the clump so the threads growing there wither and die. Meanwhile, the outer threads continue to spread, and so it is that the next crop of toadstools comes up in the form of a small ring. Each year the threads carry on growing outwards in a circle. They can't grow back towards the centre because they have already exhausted the food supply there. So the ring goes on getting bigger every year.

Many different kinds of mushroom and toadstool form fairy rings. The ring in the big picture is formed by a large fungus called a parasol mushroom. These fungi spring up in pastureland in the autumn, especially near hedge-rows, and may be as much as 25 cms high. You can recognise them very easily by their scaly cap, the wavy lines on the stalk, and the loose-fitting double ring growing near the top of the stem. The caps are egg-shaped at first, but soon flatten out to form the familiar parasol shape. Each one scatters millions of tiny spores from the gills under its cap and those falling on suitable ground grow into new toadstool threads.

8

How big is the ring?

Look for a well-formed fairy ring in a field and examine it closely. Use a good guide book to find out what kind of toadstools form your ring.

Measure the diameter of the ring and count the number of toadstools in it.

Try to go back again the next year and measure the ring again. How much has it grown in a year?

YEAR 1

YEAR 2

Melting ink-caps

Shaggy ink-cap toadstools are a familiar sight on roadside verges. Look for them in the autumn. Can you think why they are also called "lawyers' wigs"?

The ink-cap is white at first, but it soon turns black and starts to melt into an inky liquid. The toadstool's spores are in the liquid and they are carried away by flies which come to drink it.

Look at the toadstools each day. How long do they take to melt right away?

The elegant lapwing

The lapwing gets its name from the "lapping" sound that is made by its broad black and white wings as it flies along. But this handsome bird is also known by several other names. Some people call it the peewit, because that is what its call sounds like. And others call it the green plover. In some country areas it is even known as the butcher bird, because its clean white "apron" resembles the large aprons that butchers wear.

Lapwings are sociable birds and live in large flocks for much of the year. They like all kinds of grassland but are especially fond of farms. You can often see them in the fields during autumn, after the grain has been harvested. They roam through the stubble, sometimes walking and sometimes running for short distances, as they search for worms and insects. They also eat seeds and the occasional tasty leaf.

If the birds are disturbed, the whole flock may rise into the air and flap lazily around the field a couple of times before landing again. Watch the slow flapping of their wings and look for the striking black and white underside. You might even be lucky enough to see the lapwing's amazing aerial display – full of breathtaking dives and swerves. Listen also for the lapwing's well-known call when it is flying. You can hear this at night as well as by day, for the lapwing doesn't bother about time and sleeps when it likes.

The lapwing flocks break up early in the spring and each pair claims about an acre of land on which to rear its brood of young. The nest is merely a hollow in the ground, often lined with bits of grass. The female lays up to four eggs. They are brown with black spots and are very hard to see – especially on ploughed land.

Following the plough

If you see a tractor ploughing a field in the autumn or winter, you will usually see a flock of birds following behind. These birds have learned that the plough turns up lots of juicy worms and other small animals which can be easily caught and eaten. Try to find some of these creatures in the earth yourself.

The **woodpigeon** (*left*) does not follow the plough but is very common in the fields. It feeds mainly on leaves and does quite a lot of damage to young cereal plants.

Most of the black birds following the plough are **rooks**, like the one on the right. Look for the grey patch at the base of their beaks.

The **carrion crow** (*right*) follows the plough in small numbers. Look for its all-black beak to distinguish it from the rook.

The **black-headed gull** (*left*), seen here in its winter plumage, is one of the commonest birds behind the plough. It often flies well inland, many miles from the sea.

11

Among the grasses

The grasses that make up our fields and meadows look very much alike when they are not in flower. But in the summer, when the flowers finally appear, you will soon see that there are many different kinds. Perhaps you didn't even realise that grasses actually *had* flowers – because you normally see them on lawns or fields which are regularly mown or grazed. Try looking on rough hillsides and roadside verges in June. You will see masses of feathery flower spikes, some straight and some branching. Use a magnifying glass to examine them.

Grass flowers don't look like ordinary flowers though. Each individual flower is minute. It has no petals and is normally a dull colour because it doesn't need to attract insects to carry its pollen to other grasses. Instead, the pollen is merely scattered by the wind. In fact, this is what gives so many people hay fever in the height of the flowering season – the pollen in the air irritates their noses.

Look carefully at the sprays of flowers. You will see tiny stamens hanging from the scaly flower clusters or spikelets, scattering their pollen in the breeze. You will also see the feathery stigmas. These are the female parts of the flower and their job is to catch the pollen. When the right kind of pollen has been caught the flowers begin to form seeds.

Grasses which are regularly grazed or mown cannot send up flower shoots, but they are not harmed by this treatment. The more the tips are nibbled or mown, the more side shoots spring from the base. These side shoots eventually become matted together to form the turf. Have a look at these matted shoots on your lawn or in a grazed field. Compare this turf with an unmown roadside verge or a hayfield in which the grasses are allowed to grow up to flowering stage. The grasses here do not form a dense turf.

nature watch

Spiky plantains

Many other plants grow among the grasses. The **ribwort plantain** seen here is very common in all types of grassland. In grazed areas its leaves lie almost flat, but in longer grass they stand upright. Its flowers grow in brownish spikes. Each plantain spike carries lots of tiny flowers which, like those of the grasses, are pollinated by the wind. The pollen is scattered from hanging white stamens that start flowering at the bottom of the spike. That's why you'll always find just one ring of stamens on the spike which appears to move upwards day by day as a new ring of flowers opens and the lower ones wither. How many days does it take for the ring to move right up the spike?

Stamens

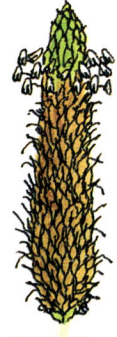

Young spike   Middle-aged spike   Old spike

Cocksfoot grass is so named because its flower heads branch out rather like a chicken's foot. It is very common on roadside verges and other rough grassland.

False oat grass can be recognised by its shiny spikelets. Each one normally contains two flowers. This grass is abundant on roadsides and rough ground.

Perennial rye grass bears its spikelets in two rows on a long stalk. Each spikelet has several flowers. It is very nutritious so is often grown for hay and pastureland.

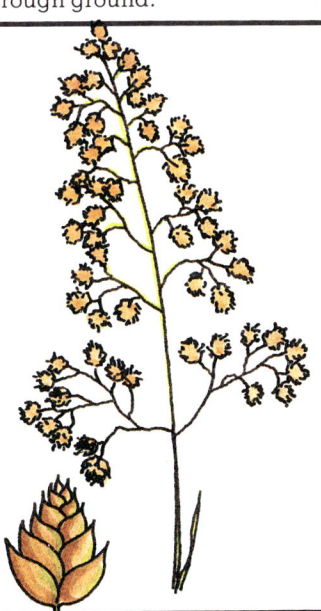

Meadow foxtail grass has dense, soft flower spikes with tightly packed spikelets. Each spikelet has just one flower. The grass is found mainly in old meadows.

Quaking grass is easily recognised by its rounded spikelets, carried on graceful branching stems. Each spikelet has several flowers. It grows mainly on the chalk downs.

Timothy grass has dense flower spikes like those of meadow foxtail, but they are much rougher to touch. Each spikelet has just one flower. It is widely grown for hay-making.

The return of the rabbit

Rabbits are so common everywhere that it is hard to imagine the fields and woods without them. But, in fact, this nearly happened in the 1950s when a disease called myxomatosis spread through Europe and killed nearly all of them. Farmers were pleased, because rabbits often do tremendous damage to crops and also eat a lot of the grass intended for the sheep and cattle. Naturalists were not so happy, however, because without rabbits to keep the turf short, lots of grassy hillsides soon became covered with bushes and many wild flowers disappeared. You can read more about these changes on page 26.

Happily, though, the rabbits did not completely disappear. Some were immune to the disease and were able to carry on breeding. So rabbit numbers gradually built up again, and in some areas they are now nearly as common as they were before myxomatosis arrived. Unless you live in a very built-up area, you shouldn't have any trouble in finding rabbits to watch. Look for them in rough grassland, woodland clearings, and also around the hedgerows on farm land. The first signs you see of rabbit activity will probably be their burrows, which are usually surrounded by bare earth. Rabbits are very sociable animals and

they like to live in large colonies. You will normally find lots of their burrows close together, forming a huge underground system called a warren.

Rabbits will sometimes feed during the day in areas where they are not disturbed by people, but it is usually best to look for them on a summer evening. If you sit quietly near the warren you can watch them feeding and playing. But remember not to stand up suddenly or make any other quick movement, for this will send the rabbits scurrying into their burrows. The first ones to see you will stamp their hind feet hard on the ground to warn the others. And, as they bound away on their short legs, their flashing white tails act as another warning of danger.

Much of the rabbits' grazing is done within about 100 metres of their burrows, unless there are hedgerows or rocks to provide shelter. So the grass close to the warren is usually very short and may be absent altogether. But as you get further from the burrows you will see that the grass begins to get longer. Ragwort, which you can see in the picture, may grow around the mouths of the burrows, and there may be stinging nettles as well. These plants manage to survive around the rabbit warren because the rabbits will not eat them.

Baby rabbits are born in special burrows, called stops, which are not connected to the main burrows. The babies are blind and naked for the first few days and their mothers regularly visit the stops to feed them.

nature detective

Rabbit or hare?

The rabbit and the brown hare both live in grassland and people often muddle them up. However, you can always recognise the hare by its longer, black-tipped ears and much longer legs. Also, the upper side of the hare's tail is black, but that of the rabbit is brown, although you don't usually see this when the animals are running.

The **rabbit** (above) is 45 cms long at the most, but the **hare** (right) can reach 65 cms in length.

Gaudy moths

If you walk across a flower-covered hill-side in summer, you will almost certainly see some black and red moths sitting quietly on the flowers. They are burnet moths, like the one on the right of the picture, and they are especially fond of knapweed and scabious flowers. If you look carefully you will see their long tongues probing among the petals, searching for nectar. You can get very close to them, and even pick them up, for they are rather lazy insects. When they do fly, they beat their wings rapidly but still only drift silently through the air.

There are several different kinds of burnet moth. The one in the picture is a 6-spot burnet – it has six red spots on each front wing. Some have only five spots and others have more complicated patterns, but the hind wings are always red with black edges. Because they are brightly coloured and fly by day, many people think that burnets are butterflies.

The burnet caterpillar, on the far right of the picture, feeds on yellow bird's-foot trefoil. When fully grown, it forms a papery cocoon on a plant stem and gradually changes into a moth. You might even see a new moth crawl out of its cocoon, if you keep your eyes open.

The moth on the left of the picture is a cinnabar moth. You might confuse it with a burnet at first, but the wing pattern is quite different and the black areas are not nearly so shiny. You might also notice that the cinnabar's antennae, or feelers, are not clubbed like those of the burnet. You can find cinnabar moths in rough grassland where the ragwort grows. The black and gold caterpillars are very common on this plant in the summer. Their bold colours warn birds that they are poisonous and unpleasant to eat.

Cinnabar caterpillar

nature detective

Butterfly or moth?

Butterflies and moths belong to the same large group of insects, and all have a covering of tiny scales on their wings. If you handle one of these insects, lots of scales will come off on your fingers. But do you know how to tell the difference between a butterfly and a moth? The best way to separate them is to look at their feelers or antennae. Butterfly antennae always have little knobs at the end. Moth antennae come in many shapes, but never have these little knobs.

Cinnabar moth

Burnet cocoon

Burnet moth

Burnet caterpillar

Burnet moth antennae *(right)* are swollen or clubbed towards the tip, but do not have obvious knobs at the end like those of butterflies.

The **cinnabar moth** *(right)* has slender antennae. Many of the smaller moths have antennae like this.

This **butterfly head** *(left)* clearly shows the knobbed antennae. Butterflies all fly by day, and this is also a useful way of telling them apart from moths.

The male **emperor moth** *(left)* has large feathery antennae with which he smells out the female. She has smaller antennae.

The slithering grass snake

The grass snake is really quite a common creature, but it is rarely seen by people. This is because it's very timid and usually slithers quietly away before it can be spotted. The grass snake knows when someone is approaching because it picks up vibrations from the ground. So if you are looking for a snake you must walk very softly. On the other hand, if you are in an area where poisonous snakes are known to live you can usually scare them away by stamping and shaking the ground as you walk along.

The best place to look for grass snakes is in damp grassland around ponds and streams. But you can also find them in hedgerows, especially those flanked by water-filled ditches. Warm, sunny days are the ideal time, for then you might find them sunbathing – snuggled against a stone or curled up at the base of a tree.

The grass snake's body may be grey, greenish or brown, but you can almost always recognise it by its yellowish collar. It will hiss loudly at you when disturbed and it may even strike out, but normally it keeps its mouth firmly closed and very rarely bites people. It is not poisonous and you can safely pick it up – if you can catch it. But if you do succeed

in getting hold of it, the snake may emit a foul-smelling liquid. This helps to protect it from enemies such as hedge-hogs and badgers. If really frightened, it will pretend to be dead by lying in the position shown in the circle below.

If you watch a snake closely you will see its tongue constantly flicking in and out. This is not the snake licking its lips, though, rather it's how it picks up the scent of its prey. It's favourite foods are frogs and toads. The toad in the picture is puffing itself up to try and trick the snake into thinking that it is much bigger than it really is. Grass snakes swim well and often catch their food in the water. They go to sleep in October, usually in a deep hole, and do not normally wake up again until March.

Lizard or snake?

nature detective

Lizards and snakes both belong to a large group of animals called *reptiles*. They all have scaly skins. But most lizards also have legs, so you can tell the two groups of creatures apart. However, there are some lizards that don't have legs, and then things are not so easy. To tell which is which you must look at the eyes: lizards all have proper eye-lids, but snakes do not so they always have their eyes open! The only legless lizard in Britain is the slow worm. We have two normal lizards and three kinds of snake. All go to sleep for the winter.

The **slow worm** *(above and right)* is a legless lizard with very smooth scales. It lives in grassy places, and feeds on slugs.

The **adder** *(above and left)* is Britain's only poisonous snake. Look for the zig-zag line on its back and the vertical pupil in the eye.

The **smooth snake** *(right)* can usually be recognised by the dark stripe running from the snout to the neck. It is not poisonous, although it bites.

The brilliant poppy

A field of scarlet poppies is certainly a brilliant sight, but it's now a much rarer one than it was 50 years ago. The poppy is a serious weed in the grain fields and hay meadows, so the farmers always try to get rid of it. That's one reason why you don't see many poppies in the fields these days, although they are still common enough on roadsides and waste land. You won't see poppies growing in dense grassland either, because their tiny seeds need more or less bare soil in which to start growth.

The common field poppy is an annual plant which starts to grow in the spring and dies in the autumn. Look for it on the roadside. Notice its hairy leaves and the buds which hang down until they are ready to open. When it's time for them to flower, they quickly grow upright and the two green sepals fall to the ground, allowing the crumpled petals to unfold. However, the petals never quite lose *all* their creases, so they always look as if they need ironing! Look also at the numerous black, pollen-filled stamens in the centre of the flower. Brush them with your finger and you will pick up a lot of pale yellow pollen. Right in the centre of the flower you will see the cup-shaped capsule in which the seeds develop after pollination. Bumble bees help carry the pollen from flower to flower. Try to watch them at work, gathering pollen with their legs as they move round inside the flower.

The poppy's seeds are very small and many are washed deep down into the soil. They remain alive there for as long as 100 years, waiting to be brought to the surface again so they can grow into bright, new plants. This is why drifts of poppies suddenly appear on roadsides and other places where soil has been churned up.

nature project

The poppy's pepper-pot

Examine a ripe, brown poppy capsule and you will see a ring of tiny holes just under the cap. It is through these that the poppy's tiny seeds escape for, as the capsule sways from side to side in the breeze, it throws the seeds out through the holes. Gently push a stalk to one side and let it go. Can you see how far some of the seeds are thrown? Try counting the seeds in a capsule. You might find well over a thousand!

nature watch

Harmful weeds

Farmers have to deal with many kinds of weed in their fields. Modern chemical sprays help them to keep the weeds under control. Some weeds, like **ragwort**, on the left, are poisonous to sheep and cattle. Others, like the **creeping thistle** on the right, are avoided because they are so prickly. They spread rapidly and take over the pasture.

Capsule

Stamen

Moles down below

You have probably never seen a mole, because this quaint little animal spends all of its life tunnelling in the ground. But you will almost certainly have seen evidence of its underground workings, as mole hills – piles of loose earth pushed up by the mole in grassland and woodland and perhaps even on your own lawn. Look at the picture below and you'll be able to see the huge front feet which the mole uses to dig its tunnels. It scrapes the soil backwards with these shovel-like feet, and every metre or so pushes it up to the surface to form a mole hill. The hill has no real entrance, although

the mole occasionally sticks its head right through the earth to the surface above. The loose earth allows air to get down into the tunnel, but the hill doesn't last for long because the soil soon gets scattered over the ground above.

Each mole lives alone in a tunnel system covering perhaps 1,000 square metres – about a quarter of the size of a football field! The animal's velvety black fur can be brushed in any direction, so the mole can move backwards and forwards in its tunnels with equal ease. These tunnels are rarely more than 50 cms deep. In fact, most are less than

25 cms below the surface and some are so shallow that you can even see a ridge where the mole has tunnelled. At intervals in the deeper tunnels the mole digs out a sleeping chamber and lines it with grass. These chambers are usually under somewhat larger mole hills. The female has her babies in a larger chamber under an even larger mound.

Moles feed almost entirely on earthworms, which they catch as they tunnel through the soil. The worms often fall right into the mole's passageways and are then easily caught. When worms are particularly numerous the mole stores them in a "larder", after biting off their heads so they can't crawl away. If the mole doesn't come back for them, the worms eventually grow new heads and escape!

The mole's subway

Look for a line of fresh mole hills when you're out walking in the fields. These will show you where the mole has been tunnelling. You might be lucky enough to see a new hill being pushed up or even the mole itself poking its head out, but this is rare. Occasionally you may find a much bigger mole hill, showing where the mole has excavated a "bedroom" in the ground and pushed up an extra large amount of soil.

Other underground dwellers

Many animals tunnel in the ground. Some use their tunnels or burrows merely to sleep in, but many actually feed under the ground as well. Some, like the mole, eat other animals, while others eat plant roots. How many burrowing animals can you think of? Two very different kinds are shown here.

The **mole cricket** (above) tunnels with its big front legs. It chews plant roots and may come out to fly in the evening. The male sits at the entrance to his burrow and "sings" to attract the female.

The **Alpine marmot** (left) sleeps in its burrow like the rabbit and feeds on grasses and other plants.

23

Which butterfly is which?

You often hear people saying that there are not as many butterflies around today as there were 20 or 30 years ago. This is true in some places, because the fields where they used to live have disappeared under roads and housing estates. But if you visit the wilder grasslands of the downs and mountain slopes you can still see many different kinds.

You will usually find lots of butterflies wherever there are lots of different kinds of flower. The flowers provide food for the adult insects, whilst their leaves feed the caterpillars. They are common in the old-fashioned hay-meadows where wild flowers grow in abundance. But modern hay fields are generally sown with the seeds of the strongest and most nutritious grasses – they contain few other flowers and few butterflies.

Make a note in your *Nature Diary* whenever you see a new kind of butterfly. Here are some you might spot in grassland.

The **meadow brown** is one of the commonest grassland butterflies. The female is more orange than the male. The caterpillar feeds on various grasses.

The **marbled white** is a strong flier of the rough grassland. It likes to feed from knapweed and scabious flowers. Its caterpillar feeds on grasses.

The **black-veined white** often has transparent wings, especially in the female. It is extremely common in scrubby places in Europe, but it doesn't live in Britain.

The **clouded yellow** is a great traveller. It comes to Britain and other parts of northern Europe for the summer. It enjoys clover fields, where its caterpillars feed.

The **common blue** occurs on all kinds of grassland. The female is brown. The caterpillars feed on bird's-foot trefoil and on the restharrow seen here.

Chalkhill blues occur only on chalk and limestone grassland because that's where their foodplant, the horseshoe vetch, grows. As with all the blues, the female is brown.

The **small heath** is common on all kinds of grassland from May until October. It is less attracted to flowers than most other butterflies. The caterpillar eats grasses.

The **grizzled skipper** keeps close to the ground, darting rapidly from one place to another. Look for it in scrubby grassland. The caterpillar feeds mainly on wild strawberry.

The **grayling** prefers drier grasslands and heathlands. It is very difficult to see when resting with its wings closed on the ground. Its caterpillar eats various grasses.

The **dark green fritillary** frequents rough grassland, including sea cliffs, and also moorland regions. It is a strong flier. Its caterpillar eats wild violets.

Invading shrubs

Fields and open spaces of green grassland are a familiar sight all over Europe.
But they are not really a natural part of the
landscape. They remain only as long as
the grass is kept short by mowing or
grazing. And as soon as this is reduced,
the fields and hillsides start to change, by
gradually returning to their original state.

The first thing that we notice is that the
grasses grow up and flower, many of them
forming large clumps. Any animals still
grazing there tend to avoid eating these
clumps. So, protected by the grasses, the
seedlings of many shrubs can grow
where they couldn't survive before.

After a few years what was once grassland becomes scrub – scattered bushes
separated by patches of grass. Some of
these invading shrubs are shown in the
picture. Birch is one of the first to get established on light soil because its winged
seeds are soon brought in by the wind.
The seeds of other shrubs are scattered
by birds which have eaten their fruits in
neighbouring woods and hedgerows.

The change to the landscape doesn't
stop there, though. For the shrubs
gradually crowd out the grasses and
other small plants. Then the seeds of trees
arrive and become established under the
protection of the shrubs. After a few years
the trees are taller than the shrubs and
kill most of them off by blocking out the
light. So it is that woods are formed.

The change from grassland to woodland is part of the process called
succession. It has taken place in many
parts of Europe ever since a disease
called myxomatosis killed off most of
the rabbits. And although the rabbits
eventually returned, they could not
nibble down the young trees and turn
the woods back to grassland again.

Dogwood

Buckthorn

Hawthorn

Birch

Privet

Guelder rose

27

The hovering hunter

The kestrel spends a great deal of its time hovering in the air. Instead of flying along, it beats its wings rapidly and spreads out its fan-like tail to keep itself in one place, high above the earth. Even in very windy weather this beautiful bird can hold its position over one spot on the ground for as long as five minutes. But the hovering is not for fun. The kestrel is a bird of prey and hovering is all part of the serious business of hunting. Field voles are its favourite food and the kestrel needs to catch at least two of them every day to keep itself alive. And when it has a mate and babies to feed, it needs to catch even more.

When it's out hunting, the kestrel hovers up to 30 metres above the ground, using its sharp eyes to scan the surface for the slightest movement. Then, when it spots its victim, it glides silently down until it is just above the ground, pulls back its wings and drops suddenly onto its prey. Look for kestrels on open grassland and moors and also in town parks. You can also see them hovering over motorway verges.

The kestrel's dinner

Although the kestrel's main prey is the field vole, it will eat many other animals, including worms and insects. Some of its regular victims are shown here. Have you seen a kestrel catch any of these?

The bird on the right is a male kestrel. The female has no grey on her head or tail. You can often see kestrels resting on fences and telegraph poles.

Burying beetles

Have you ever wondered why you rarely see dead animals in the countryside? One of the reasons is that when small animals become old or ill they are easily caught and eaten by their enemies. But another very important reason is that nature provides a ready-made army of scavengers to get rid of dead creatures. You can think of these scavengers as nature's dustmen, clearing up the rubbish. Lots of different kinds of animals join in this work, but some of the most interesting are the burying beetles which you can see working away on the right. Some of the burying beetles are dressed entirely in black, but most of them are black with orange stripes.

The burying beetles are good fliers and buzz about, smelling out dead animals with the aid of their antennae. If you look at the antennae you will see that they have clubbed tips, which are specially designed to pick up scent. The beetles usually work in pairs. When the first one arrives at a carcase it defends it and chases other beetles away until a mate arrives. Then the pair start to bury the carcase by digging the soil away from underneath it.

They work so quickly that, in light soil, a small bird or a mouse can be completely buried in just an hour! The beetles may eat some of the meat themselves, but the real purpose of burying the carcase is to provide a larder for their youngsters. For, once the animal is buried, the female beetle lays her eggs in a small chamber close by and the grubs feed on the meat when they hatch.

If you find a dead creature, turn it carefully over with a stick to see if there are any burying beetles hiding underneath it. You will probably find lots of maggots too.

nature detective

Name that beetle!

Many beetles bury dung instead of dead animals, and so play an important role in keeping the countryside clean. They bury the dung with their broad front legs and lay their eggs in it. The buried dung remains moist for a long time so the beetle grubs can feed on it for several months. The most famous of these dung beetles are the scarabs. They roll large balls of dung about until they find suitable places in which to bury them. Scarabs live in warm regions. There are no real scarabs in Britain, although several live in southern Europe.

A **scarab beetle** (left) rolls its ball of dung along with its hind legs. It always moves backwards.

The **minotaur beetle** (right) can be found on dry grassland. It buries rabbit dung in a deep burrow.

The **dor beetle** (right), often called the lousy watchman or dumble-dor, tunnels underneath cow pats and drags large quantities down into the ground.

The **bloody-nose beetle** (left) resembles the dor beetle, but it does not eat dung. When alarmed it exudes blood from its mouth.

The thrush's anvil

If you hear a loud tapping sound when you're walking in the countryside it may be a song thrush at work at its anvil. The bird is not, of course, using its "anvil" to shape steel like a blacksmith, but is, in fact, dealing with its favourite food – the snail. This bird will search diligently among the vegetation until it finds a suitable victim, and will then carry it to a convenient stone. To get at the snail's soft, juicy body, the thrush batters it against the stone until its shell breaks into several pieces. The thrush can then settle down to its tasty meal!

Most thrushes have one or two favourite stones which they use to break open nearly all their snails. You can find these anvils all over the place – in woods, hedgerows and gardens, as well as on the grassland. When you find one it is worth waiting around for the thrush to return with its next meal. Then you can see exactly how it breaks open the snail's shell. Don't sit too close to the anvil, though, or the birds might go elsewhere – get further back and use your binoculars if possible.

Try removing all the shell fragments from around the anvil when the bird has gone, and then visit the same spot after a day or two has passed. Collect the shell pieces again and you will get some idea of how many snails the thrush eats in a day. Also, try searching the surrounding grassland for living snails. Unless it has been raining, you will find it difficult to spot them and will realise how good the thrush's eyes are.

Of course, the song thrush does not live entirely on snails. Earthworms, caterpillars and berries are its other major foods. It eats snails mainly in the summer, before the new berry crop is ripe.

nature detective

Winter thrushes

The song thrush has several close relatives, including the blackbird and the mistle thrush. The latter is larger and greyer than the song thrush and lives mainly in the woods, while the familiar blackbird can be seen almost everywhere. Two other members of the thrush family – the fieldfare and the redwing – breed in northern Europe and fly south to Britain and other areas for the winter. Both can be seen foraging in the fields, but they are especially noticeable in the hedgerows, where they feed on haws and other fruits throughout the winter.

Banded snails

The majority of the shells found around the thrush's anvil belong to two species known as banded snails. One kind has a white lip and one has a brown lip, but otherwise they are very similar. Most of the banded snails living on the grassland are yellow in colour, and may or may not have brown bands. In the spring and early summer, when the grass is bright green, the unbanded snails are well camouflaged so the thrushes take mainly the banded ones. Later in the summer, when the grasses are turning brown, the banded shells are harder to see and so the thrushes take more of the unbanded kind. If you look at an anvil at different times of year you will see this.

Banded snails have up to five bands on each whorl, but the bands are not all the same width. Try making a collection of empty shells to show their different patterns.

In this shell the five bands have all joined up to give the shell a completely brown appearance. Shells like this are found mainly in woodland. Can you think why?

This shell has no bands at all and would be difficult to spot in fresh green grass. Snails living in woodlands are often pink instead of yellow so they blend in with their surroundings.

The **redwing** (right) gets its name from the rust-coloured patch on its side.

The **fieldfare** (left) is a little larger than the redwing and has a distinctly grey head and rump.

Common and colourful

Few flowers grow in heavily grazed pastures because they are constantly trampled on or eaten by grazing animals. But the rougher grasslands of hillsides are always full of flowers in the summer.

Where there is moderate grazing the plants are all quite short, their leaves generally forming mats or rosettes at ground level where they are relatively safe from grazers. The taller plants can normally grow only where there is little or no grazing. Visit some rough grassland and mark out a square, measuring a metre along each side. Count the number of different flowers growing in the square. You will be surprised how many there are. Some of the commoner kinds are illustrated below.

① The **ox-eye daisy** grows in rough grassland and is often found on roadside verges. It flowers from May to September and each flower may be 50 mm across.

② The **common rockrose** is a low-growing plant which often forms mats on ant hills. It grows on chalk and limestone hills and flowers from May to September. Despite its name, it is not a true rose.

③ **Meadow clary** is a relative of the mint and the deadnettle. It grows on chalk and limestone grassland and flowers in June and July.

④ **Wild thyme** is a low-growing plant which, like the rockrose, often grows on ant hills. It prefers dry grassland and flowers from June to September.

⑤ **Field scabious** grows on dry grass-land of all kinds and flowers from June to October. The flower heads are up to 40 mm across. There are several similar, but smaller, kinds of scabious.

⑥ **Salad burnet** grows on dry grass-land, especially on chalk and limestone, and flowers from May to September. The quaint round flower heads have no petals. The leaves taste of cucumber.

⑦ **Meadow cranesbill** is a tall and very beautiful plant of limestone soils, where it flowers from June to September In Britain, it is most common in the north.

⑧ **Greater knapweed** flowers on road-sides and other rough, grassy places from June to September. Black knapweed has smaller flowers and smoother leaves.

⑨ **Bird's-foot trefoil** gets its name because its seed pods spread out like a bird's toes. It flowers all summer in grassy and rocky places.

nature project

Pressing flowers

You can collect some of the commoner wild flowers and preserve them by pressing them between sheets of blotting paper until they are dry. Two sheets of hardboard screwed together make a useful press. Holes drilled in them will help the moisture to escape.

1 Arrange your flowers neatly on the paper and cover them with another sheet. You can add several such layers before closing the press. Leave it for several weeks to dry the plants.

2 Remove your plants from the press and mount them in a scrap book or on sheets of plain paper. Small strips of gummed paper are best for holding the plants in place. Label each plant with its name, and the date and place where you found it. Keep the collection in a dry place. Never pick flowers from plants that you think might be rare – by doing so you deprive other people of a chance of seeing them. You also stop the plant from scattering seeds – and so it will become rarer still. Make a collection only of common flowers.

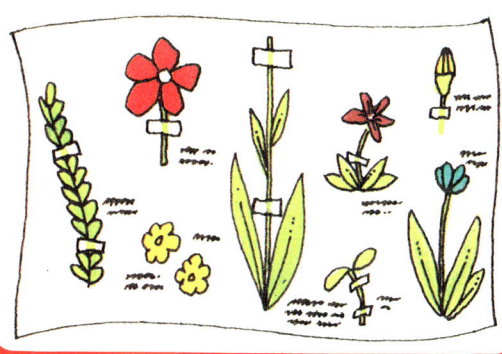

Singing grasshoppers

You can't walk very far through rough grassland in the summer without hearing the chirping song of the grasshopper. We call it a song, but really it is a series of buzzing sounds.

Most grasshoppers are green and brown and very hard to see when they're in the grass, but if you follow the sounds you will soon find these noisy insects. Try walking very carefully towards the sound when you hear it and you may even be able to see how the grasshopper actually produces his song.

You will see him moving his big hind legs up and down, rubbing them against his wings. This makes a noise because the inner surface of each leg has a row of tiny pegs on it. And as these pegs pass over a hard vein on the wing, they make the buzzing sound. In fact, you can imitate the sound yourself by drawing the teeth of a comb over your finger nail. Of course, the grasshopper's pegs are too small for you to see without a good magnifying glass, but you can see them in the enlargement in the picture.

The noise made by the grasshopper is, in fact, a mating call made only by the male insect to attract a mate. So if you watch patiently you might see the female approach. She is larger than the male. Remember, though, not to let your shadow fall on the singing male. If you do, he will probably stop singing and hop away. He usually stops when the sun goes in.

Grasshoppers lay their eggs around the bases of grasses. The eggs hatch in spring and out pop the babies. Young grasshoppers look like the adults but have no wings at first. They feed almost entirely on grass and are fully grown from July onwards.

nature detective

Grasshopper or cricket?

Grasshoppers and crickets are closely related, but it's quite easy to tell which is which. The **grasshopper** (below) has short antennae, but crickets have very long ones – in fact, they're often even longer than the cricket's body.

Having grasshoppers to stay

Grasshoppers are very easy to keep at home. A large sweet jar with a muslin cover will make a fine house for them if you don't have a proper cage. And all they need is fresh grass every day.

1 First, you must catch your grasshoppers – either by using a net or by lowering a glass tube gently over them. This is surprisingly easy: the insects always leap upwards, and usually jump into the tube.

2 Next, put a layer of sand in the cage – you must remember to moisten it each day. Add a piece of turf if you can. The lamp is not really necessary, but it warms the insects and they are more likely to sing.

3 Add some taller pieces of grass for the grasshoppers to climb, and then put the insects into the cage. Don't put the lamp too close or the cage will become too hot.

4 Watch the grasshoppers going about their daily lives. Listen to their songs: can you spot the differences? See how the insects use their big back legs to leap from one grass blade to another.

The **field cricket** (below) lives in a burrow in grassland. You may hear the male singing at the entrance to his home in sunny weather. Like all the crickets, he sings by rubbing his wings together. The female field cricket has a long, needle-like spine at her hind end. She uses this to lay eggs in the ground. There are many other kinds of cricket. Most of them sing at night.

Flying high, singing loud

The skylark is a real lover of open spaces. So, if you want to see it, you will have to visit the farmlands or the grassy hills and moorlands, or perhaps even the coastal dunes and marshes. The bird is very well named, for the male spends a great deal of his time high in the sky, pouring out his cheerful, bubbling song. He will fly up and up, away from his nest on the ground, singing all the time. In fact, he sometimes flies so high that he reaches heights of 300 metres or more. At such times, he is scarcely visible, but his shrill song can be easily heard and this is how he defends his nest and territory. Most small birds sing from trees and hedgerows, but the skylark rarely goes near them. If he is not in the air, he usually has both his small feet firmly on the ground!

If you see a male hovering and singing in the air you can be fairly certain that his nest is immediately below him, but you should never try to find it. This will not only frighten the birds, but the nest is usually so well camouflaged that you are also likely to tread on it by mistake.

The skylark's nest is built with grass and hair and is most often sited in a small hollow in the ground – often among quite tall grasses. The parent birds are quite happy nesting among wheat and other farm crops and usually manage to rear two or even three broods before the crops are harvested. Each brood contains three or four chicks which hatch from mottled eggs like those in the picture. The eggs are incubated by the mother bird alone and 10 days after hatching the chicks finally leave the nest. They cannot fly, though. It takes them another 10 days to learn the aerobatic skills of their parents.

Skylarks feed on seeds and insects and remain in the fields throughout the year. However, those that breed in the far north will fly south for the winter.

Skylark look-alikes

nature detective

The **yellowhammer** *(below)* is very common on farmland but, unlike the skylark, it also likes the hedge-rows. Its song is said to sound like someone singing "a little bit of bread and no chee-ee-ee-se". See if you can identify the yellowhammer's strange request next time you're out walking.

The **meadow pipit** *(below)* lives in all kinds of rough grassland and is quite similar to the skylark but, at about 14.5 cms long, it is a little smaller. It also has a more slender beak. Can you see any other differences? Like the skylark, it usually avoids settling in trees, and it utters a tinkling song as it flies along. You can often tell a meadow pipit by the way it flies – going up and down, up and down.

Pheasants abroad!

You are most likely to see the pheasant strutting through the fields – either in the spring when the crops are short, or after the autumn harvest. You might also see this handsome bird crossing country roads. It usually walks slowly with its head held proudly in the air, but it may run off if a car approaches and, if it is really scared, it will take off with a rapid whirring of its wings and a loud crowing sound.

In fact, the pheasant is quite a noisy bird altogether. It lives mainly on farmland and in light woodland where it nests in the spring. You can often hear the cock birds making a lot of noise at this time of year – crowing and cackling almost like farmyard chickens.

The male pheasant is smartly and brightly dressed, as you can see from the picture. His colours vary a good deal and are brightest in the spring when the birds are courting. Many of the males have a white collar. The female, on the right of the picture, is always brown. She lays up to 15 eggs in a simple grass-lined hollow in the ground. Both birds eat seeds and young leaves and also catch lots of wireworms and other soil-dwelling insects.

Pheasants have not always lived in Europe. They were brought here from southern Asia over 1,000 years ago to provide food for the people. Even today, most of the pheasants that you see in the fields will have been specially reared by landowners. Small areas of woodland are set aside for the birds to nest in, and gamekeepers are sometimes employed to look after them. But when the birds grow up in the autumn, most of them are shot and eaten. However, enough birds are always left to provide the eggs for the next year's crop.

nature watch

The plump partridge

The partridge likes to live on farmland, especially among cereals and other crops. It is related to the pheasant, but hasn't got a long tail like its bigger cousin. If a partridge is disturbed in the grass it will often just run away. But at other times it will sit very still until the danger passes. If you walk too close to a crouching bird, though, it may suddenly fly up and give out a loud, cackling call which can be very startling. The bird very soon lands again and it can be very difficult to pick out on the ground. It *never* perches in trees.

Two kinds of partridge are common in Britain – the **common** or **grey partridge** *(below left)* and the **red-legged partridge** *(below right)*. How many differences can you spot between the two birds? Both have rust-red tail feathers which you can see when they fly *(right)*. And both birds eat seeds, leaves, and an assortment of insects and other small animals. For much of the summer and autumn they roam through the fields in small groups known as *coveys*.

Picture index

Panel index